Contents

Abstract

The 1995 Khobar Towers bombing and recent embassy bombings in Africa once again illustrated the threat faced by Americans, and in particular US military personnel, as a result of terrorist activity. These incidents stimulated renewed attention, literature, and efforts concerning the protection of U.S. persons overseas. Unfortunately, until recently, much less attention has been paid to terrorist threats faced inside the U.S. With a few notable exceptions (World Trade Center, Oklahoma City, etc.), the U.S. has been largely immune from terrorism on its soil. A premise of this research project is that the immunity will end in the future, sooner rather than later. Will USAF personnel be prepared for future terrorism in the U.S. or, as suspected, has the small number of domestic terrorist attacks contributed to less than optimal levels of security awareness? Alertness and security awareness have proven helpful to interdicting terrorist attacks and decreasing the number of casualties when attacks do occur (for example, the actions of an alert Security Policeman are credited with helping decrease fatalities in the Khobar Towers bombing). This project will discuss the issue of security awareness on the part of USAF personnel. Whether it be homegrown extremist "militia" type groups who fear government "repression" or international radical Islamic groups who oppose perceived Western/American decadence and U.S. encroachment in the Islamic world, the threat of terrorism on U.S. soil has increased in recent years. A key to solving a problem is understanding the problem. Thus, this project will attempt to identify and describe the likely sources of terrorism that could impact USAF resources in the U.S. Additionally, ideas will be offered to help raise awareness of USAF personnel and facilitate increased preparedness for future terrorism in the U.S. The key to stimulating and sustaining high levels of security awareness is acceptance by the populace that a problem exists. Programs such as recurring force protection "town meetings," an enhanced terrorist threat briefing program for CONUS-based US personnel, use of force protection newsletters, and innovative use of the internet, are areas to be explored for helping USAF personnel accept that the threat of terrorism exists and there is a real need for increased awareness.

Chapter 1

Introduction

Hostility toward America is a religious duty, and we hope to be rewarded for it by God...God knows that we have been pleased at the killing of American soldiers

—Osama bin Laden, Dec 1998

Why Talk About Terrorism?

Compared to other countries, the United States has enjoyed a relatively low level of terrorist violence on its own soil. Luckily, incidents such as the World Trade Center bombing and the attack on the Murrah Federal Building in Oklahoma City have been fairly infrequent. Given this historical lack of terrorism, should Americans and in particular, members of the United States Air Force (USAF), be concerned about future acts of terrorism inside the Continental United States (CONUS)? An October 1998 USA Today/CNN/Gallup poll indicated 70% of poll respondents expected the threat of terrorism to be worse in the future than it is today.[1] The above cited quote from Saudi dissident and terrorist financier Osama bin Laden should also provide an answer to the question of need for concern about terrorism. Further indication of the increased threat can be seen in President Clinton's January 1999 request for $2.8 billion to help the United States guard against terrorist attacks via biological, chemical or computer means.[2] The goal of this project is not to overestimate the potential threat to USAF personnel and resources or present a "sky is falling" viewpoint. Nor is this project intended to stimulate undue paranoia. Still, evidence is abundant to illustrate that despite the historically low number of terrorist acts on American soil, the potential for major terrorist attacks in CONUS has increased in recent years. The end of the Cold War caused the U.S. threat focus to change from one with a relatively clear threat, the Soviet Union, to a more unstable world with a diverse array of potential threats. As the sole remaining superpower and with its perceived role as the "world's policeman," America will often be the lightning rod for animosity by groups opposed to our government's policies. These groups could be both international and domestic terrorist organizations. As the enforcer of U.S. policy, American military forces could become a primary target for terrorist retribution. Further, the propaganda value of striking a CONUS military target could prove to be a tempting lure for various groups. Given this theory of increased potential for terrorism inside the U.S., the goal of this project will be to describe the likely sources of terrorism that could impact USAF personnel and resources in America. Additionally, the issue of USAF security awareness will be discussed as awareness is viewed as the key tool for interdicting terrorist acts, or at a minimum decreasing terrorist damage. Finally, suggestions to increase the general security awareness of USAF personnel will be offered.

While attempting to present a comprehensive discussion about terrorism implications for the USAF, this study will by design have certain limitations. First, the project is based on unclassified information. The addition of classified intelligence information would obviously enhance the presentation of the true threat faced by America and possibly make more readers "stand up and take notice." However, the unclassified format will help achieve the goal of increasing awareness by widening the potential audience. Further, the author is confident in the fact that enough open source and unclassified information is readily available to paint an accurate and thought-provoking picture of the current threat environment.

A second limitation involves the scope of the study. This project's focus centers on the terrorist threat in CONUS. The 1995 Khobar Towers bombing in Saudi Arabia and the 1998 embassy bombings in Kenya and Tanzania adequately illustrate the continued threat that U.S. military personnel face overseas. Additionally, while predicting increased CONUS terrorism in the future, the author understands that attacks overseas will probably continue to be a primary venue of choice due to the increased potential for the perpetrators to escape capture. However, since security awareness is, by nature of the environment, generally higher overseas, this study will focus on increasing awareness of CONUS personnel and their dependents. Thus, this focus will hopefully help fill a perceived gap in literature regarding CONUS terrorism and its potential impact on USAF personnel and resources.

Before proceeding, presentation of a definition of terrorism is essential for helping the reader understand the varied dimensions of the problem. Terrorism definitions vary from agency to agency, but respected terrorism expert Bruce Hoffman compliments the following Department of Defense (DoD) definition as being more complete than others:

> The unlawful use of – or threatened use of – force or violence against individuals or property to coerce or intimidate governments or societies, often to achieve political, religious, or ideological objectives.[3]

As Hoffman notes, this definition is unique from others in that it includes both actual violence and the threat of violence. As recent hoax letters purportedly containing anthrax (discussed in detail later) illustrate, violent acts do not actually have to be carried out, to cause fear and terror in a society. The definition is also important for purposes of this study because it encompasses a wider range of terrorist objectives (*political, religious, or ideological*) than typical definitions. Due to the current media attention given to Islamic fundamentalist extremists such as Osama bin Laden, Americans are probably most familiar with religious extremist objectives as the primary terrorist motivation. For one to have a complete understanding of why individuals or groups commit terrorist acts and thus be better prepared to deter terrorism, attention must be paid to all these possible motivations. Political, religious and ideological terrorists act differently from each other and deterrence requires understanding exactly who and what you are confronting.

As noted, the goal of this project is not to capriciously inflame fears through inflammatory predictions about terrorist onslaughts in the United States. However, through experience as a member of the Air Force Office of Special Investigations (AFOSI), the author does have personal concerns about the state of security awareness on the part of USAF personnel and their dependents. (NOTE: All information contained in this report is the product of the author's research, perceptions and opinion, and thus, does not necessarily reflect official AFOSI views or policies) Such concerns stem from events such as giving antiterrorist briefings and seeing members of the audience being clearly disinterested in the information provided. Additionally, how many of us have bristled at being delayed due to increased security checks at USAF entrance gates? The next time it occurs, perhaps readers of this paper will remember these checks are necessary due to the nature of the threats we face and to maintain a high level of security. The goal of AFOSI and USAF Security Forces is to increase the security posture of the installation to protect

USAF personnel and their families. This should be the goal of all USAF personnel as the

potential cost of a poor security environment is much too high a price to pay.

Notes

[1] Susan Page, "Americans expect good, bad and catastrophic," *USA Today*, 13 Oct 98, sec A, p. 7A.

[2] CNN, "Clinton proposes anti-terrorism plan," 22 Jan 99, [news on line]; available from http://www.cnn.com/ALLPOLITICS/stories/1999/01/22/clinton.terrorism/; Internet; accessed 22 Jan 99.

[3] Bruce Hoffman, *Inside Terrorism* (Columbia: Columbia University Press, 1998), 38.

Chapter 2

Primary CONUS Terrorist Threats

The clock is ticking/We are Revolution 2000/Within 6 months we will strike at Edwards.

—Jan 97 Threat letter received at Edwards AFB

Domestic Groups

The above threat is just one of hundreds received each year at USAF installations. Fortunately, the vast majority of these threats are simply nuisances or hoaxes. Still, the letter provides a starting point for a discussion about the various types of groups that pose a potential threat to USAF resources. As discussed earlier, the motivations for these groups run the gamut of the political, religious, and ideological spectrums. The threat ranges from the more familiar militia groups to the possibility of a single individual as described later. Since the Oklahoma City bombing, particular attention has been paid to "Patriot" and militia-type groups. In general, these groups fear unlawful government intervention into their lives and encroachment upon individual rights. Certain elements also fear that the U.S. will fall prey to a "New World Order" in which national sovereignty will be overtaken by the United Nations or foreign military forces. With some comprised of former military members, various groups stockpile large amounts of weapons and explosives, and make it clear they are preparing for future conflict. U.S. military members have been recruited for these groups due to their weapons training and

6

potential ability to provide access to weapons. While not conclusively linked to a particular militia group, convicted Oklahoma City bomber Timothy McVeigh presents a good example of the anti-government mindset of members of these groups.

Estimates vary widely about the number of militia type groups and their membership totals. One Federal Bureau of Investigation (FBI) estimate stated that tens of thousands of Americans are currently active in various anti-government groups, with several hundred being labeled as "hard core" extremists. In 1997, the Southern Poverty Law Center (SPLC) identified 523 active "Patriot" groups, with 221 of these being militia groups.[1] Particular attention must be paid to these groups as the year 2000 approaches because some view the new millennium as an apocalyptic time of potential confrontation. Thus, as we near the new year and beyond, USAF personnel (and all Americans for that matter) should stay aware of their surroundings and remain alert for suspicious individuals or packages. Paranoia is unwarranted, but good security awareness, especially on government installations or in government buildings, could mean the difference between life and death.

Although typically not violent like other groups, certain environmentalist and animal rights organizations also pose a potential threat to USAF resources. In recent months, there have been indications some of these groups might be inclined to use violence to popularize their causes. In Oct 98, a group calling itself the Earth Liberation Front (ELF), claimed credit for a fire at a Vail, Colorado ski resort. In a claim letter, the ELF said they conducted the arson to "stop the destruction of natural habitat and the exploitation of the environment."[2] The fire caused an estimated $12 million damage and became the costliest act of ecoterrorism in America. The ELF previously took partial credit for a fire at an U.S. Agriculture Department animal research facility in Olympia, Washington.[3]

In the past 20 years, more than 1500 attacks by environmentalist groups have occurred.[4] Some of these attacks have included the use of explosives. While primarily concentrating on private companies, these groups have on occasion targeted U.S. military installations for demonstrations, trespass, and acts of vandalism. For instance, in Oct 98, an animal rights group objected to USAF plans to conduct anti-mine explosives tests on Florida Panhandle beaches owned by Eglin Air Force Base because they could "disturb and harass" dolphins.[5] Should environmentalist groups continue to move toward more extreme expressions of protest, the threat to USAF resources could increase.

Another category of potential indigenous terrorist threats includes that coming from Puerto Rican terrorist groups. Most people probably do not realize that between 1982 and 1994, approximately 44% of the terrorist incidents committed in the U.S. and its territories were attributed to Puerto Rican terrorist groups.[6] These groups will use violence to attain their objective of Puerto Rico's liberation from the U.S. The Puerto Rico-based Macheteros (the most violent group) and the Armed Forces for Puerto Rican National Liberation (FALN), a clandestine group based in Chicago, are examples of the Puerto Rican terrorist organizations.[7] Puerto Rican groups have committed murders, armed robberies, thefts of weapons, and bombings of U.S. government buildings and U.S. military facilities. While major violent acts by these groups have not occurred as often in recent years as in the 1980's and early 1990's, they remain a potential threat to U.S. personnel and resources.

Other criminal elements could pose a future terrorist threat as well. Military members have been found to be members of notorious criminal gangs such as the Crips and Bloods. If in the future military members suffer punishment for gang-related activities, reprisals could occur. Also, should the U.S. military be required to increase assistance to anti-drug efforts, violence could be directed at military personnel or resources. Since criminal groups generally have easy access to weapons and are often very violent in nature, they are a threat that should not be easily discounted.

A final potential indigenous source of terrorism comes from individual psychopaths such as Theodore Kaczynski, the so-called Unabomber. This is perhaps the hardest group to confront, as they are usually difficult to interdict. The following quote from Robert Blitzer, FBI Chief of Domestic Terrorism and Counterterrorism Planning, illustrates the threat,

> We're seeing lone individuals engaging in either hoaxes or actual cases. These are the people that I'm most afraid of, the people capable of doing something like another Oklahoma City bomb. It doesn't take but one or two people to put a major bomb like that together. The ability of law enforcement to discover and prevent that kind of an act, absent help from someone who knows what they're up to, is very slim…We've had guys playing with [the deadly toxin] ricin and we've had some anthrax threat cases.[8]

While these psychopaths can be harder to deter and interdict, the Unabomber case illustrates a good example of how proper awareness can safe lives. Many of the Unabomber's victims handled or opened suspicious packages or envelopes that contained explosives. Thinking before acting could have saved lives and injuries.

International Groups

Many experts believe the international terrorist threat to the U.S. has increased in recent years and will continue for the foreseeable future. Furthermore, events such as U.S. military strikes on rogue nations increase the motivation of international terrorists to carry out revenge attacks against American targets. Countries such as Iran, Iraq, Syria, Sudan, and Libya maintain their anti-U.S. stance and could sponsor attacks if so desired. September 1998 press reports indicate that in late 1990, Saddam Hussein commanded as many as 200 terrorist followers to carry out anti-US attacks across the world, some with the plans to attack inside the U.S.[9] Exemplary intelligence and law enforcement work interdicted Saddam's intentions, but Americans should not assume that similar terrorist efforts might not be tried in the future.

International extremist groups also pose credible threats to U.S. resources. What makes these organizations particularly dangerous is that while they might conduct attacks on behalf of rogue states, they do not fall under the control of such states. Groups such as Lebanese Hizballah, Egyptian Islamic Group (IG), and the Palestinian Hamas have infrastructures inside America that support fundraising, personnel, and training (Hamas and Hizballah even have Internet homepages that include propaganda and recruiting information).[10] These groups could very easily support attacks inside the U.S. Similarly, radical Islamic extremists like Osama bin Laden, and supporters of the imprisoned Sheikh Omar Abdel Rahman have the mentality and the resources to attack U.S. targets. Of particular concern are reports that bin Laden has for several years been attempting to obtain nuclear and chemical weapons.[11] A disturbing example of the presence of international extremist groups in CONUS is the September 1998 arrest of a former U.S.

Army sergeant on charges he trained Islamic militants linked to bin Laden. The Egyptian-born individual came to the U.S. in 1985 and served three years in our military before receiving an honorable discharge in 1989.[12] This type of extremist terrorist group is often harder to confront because they usually work in small cells to increase their operational security. One thing is clear--the 1993 World Trade Center bombing clearly illustrated the fact these groups can bring terrorism to our soil.

Similar to domestic crime groups, international organized crime elements could at some point decide it is in their interest to conduct attacks inside America. Elements like the Russian Mafia or Latin American drug cartels could target U.S. military personnel or resources should they be perceived as lending too much support to anti-crime and anti-narcotic efforts.

Terrorist Modus Operandi

In general, terrorist modus operandi includes bombings, assassinations, kidnappings, sabotage, and threats of such acts. Bombings, including letter bombs, are the most frequently used terrorist method in the U.S. Compared to the 1970's and 1980's, in recent years, the overall number of successful terrorist incidents in CONUS has generally decreased (reasons for this decrease vary according to scholars). Unfortunately, the willingness of radical extremists to cause mass casualties appears to have increased. Incidents such as the World Trade Center and Oklahoma City bombings, as well as unsuccessful plots to bomb the United Nations building, FBI Office, and the Lincoln and Holland Tunnels in New York City, show the willingness of certain groups to kill large numbers of innocent Americans. It should also be pointed out these incidents were perpetrated by extremist groups with widely divergent ideologies (Islamic extremists versus American right-wing extremists). Thus, American society and law enforcement must confront a complicated, varied threat environment. One common denominator of all these plots is the perpetrators had to conduct some level of pre-operational surveillance, planning, and equipping for the attacks. It is in these phases that alert individuals can often provide information to law enforcement authorities that can interdict the attacks. Should USAF installations be targeted, military personnel and dependents can help interdict violence by being alert during pre-operational activities.

Terrorist Proximity to USAF Installations

An unfortunate consequence of the freedom enjoyed in America is the ease in which those with bad intentions can travel the country to carry out criminal acts. International and domestic transportation systems make it easy for state-sponsored terrorists to strike at perceived adversaries anywhere in the world. Domestic terrorists rely on modern transportation as well. For instance, in the 1980's, members of the United Freedom Front resided in Ohio, but traveled to New Jersey, New York, Connecticut and Massachusetts to carry out bank robberies, collect intelligence and bomb targets.[13] In addition to how modern transportation can bring terrorists closer to their targets, a quick analysis of literature indicates the presence of numerous anti-government groups in proximity to USAF installations. Almost every state in CONUS has the presence of some type of active militia/patriot groups. Further, states with multiple USAF installations, such as Texas, California, Florida, Arizona, North Carolina and South Carolina are all estimated to have over 20 of these types of groups. This is not to say all the groups are actively planning anti-US terrorist acts, but it illustrates the need for active security awareness programs. Since 1996, incidents (including bombings and planned violent attacks) involving violence-prone militia groups have occurred near Fairchild AFB, WA, Beale AFB, CA, and Luke AFB, AZ.[14]. These incidents did not involve targeting of the installations, but they did present a potential collateral threat to USAF personnel and dependents.   As previously stated, international terrorist groups such as Hizballah, Hamas, and the Islamic Group maintain an infrastructure inside America and ease of travel would facilitate anti-military terrorism on the part of these organizations should they so desire.

Notes

[1] Southern Poverty Law Center, Militia Task Force, "Active Patriot Groups," [journal on line]; available from http://www.splcenter.org/klanwatch/patriotlst.html; Internet; accessed 13 Dec 98.

[2] Associated Press, "Nature attacks on rise," *Montgomery Advertiser,* 23 October 1998, sec A, 4A.

[3] Michael Satchell, "An eco-war widens," *U.S. News and World Report*, 2 Nov 98, 36.

[4] USA Today, Associated Press, "Animal rights activists step up campaigns," [journal on line]; available from http://www.usatoday.com/news/ndsfri06htm; Internet; accessed 23 Oct 98.

[5] Associated Press, "Animal-rights group objects to tests," *Montgomery Advertiser*, 24 Oct 98, sec A, 8A.

[6] Louis J. Freeh, "Statement of Louis J. Freeh, Director, Federal Bureau of Investigation, Before the Senate Appropriations Committee Hearing on Counterterrorism United States Senate, May 13, 1997" FBI Homepage [on line]; available from http://www.fbi.gov; Internet, accessed 13 Nov 98, 5.

[7] Ibid., 6.

[8] Robert Blitzer, "Fighting Terrorism: Leading FBI Official Discusses Domestic Terrorism," *Southern Poverty Law Center*, Intelligence Report, Fall 1998, SPLC Homepage [on line]; available from http://www.splcenter.org/klanwatch/kw-4h2.html; Internet, accessed 13 Dec 98, 2.

[9] M.J. Zuckerman, "Iraq's hit squads stopped by U.S. during Gulf War," *USA Today*, 23 Sep 98, sec A, 2A.

[10] Dale Watson, "Statement of Dale Watson, Chief International Terrorism Section, National Security Division, Federal Bureau of Investigation, Before the Senate Judiciary Committee, Subcommittee on Technology, Terrorism, and Government Information United States Senate, February 24, 1998" FBI Homepage [on line]; available from http://www.fbi.gov; Internet, accessed 13 Nov 98, 2-4.

[11] Kevin Whitelaw, "Bin Laden plot gets thicker," *U.S. News and World Report*, 5 Oct 98, 12.

Notes

[12] Associated Press, "Sergeant charged with aiding terrorists," *Montgomery Advertiser*, 31 Oct 98, sec A, 3A.

[13] Karl A. Seger, *The Antiterrorism Handbook*, (Novato, CA: Presidio Press, 1990), 16

[14] David E. Kaplan, "Terrorism Threats at Home," *U.S. News and World Report*, 29 Dec 97, 22.

Chapter 3

Short History of CONUS Terrorism

Congradulations (sic)...you are now the new host of the terminal virus bacillus cutaneous anthracis, aka: ANTHRAX!

—Feb 99 Anthrax hoax letter

Historically, the U.S. has been the target of over 32% of all terrorist attacks worldwide, second to Israel.[1] Between 1980 and 1993, 299 confirmed terrorist incidents and 46 suspected terrorist incidents occurred inside the U.S.[2] Incidents such as the World Trade Center and Olympic Park bombings are well known. The following information provides a short history of relatively recent significant terrorist-related acts in CONUS, with additional emphasis on incidents in proximity to, or actually targeting, US military or government installations:

-Apr 95: Oklahoma City, OK (near Tinker AFB) - Bombing of Murrah Federal Building

-Apr-Jul 96: Spokane, WA (near Fairchild AFB) – White supremacists commit bank robberies and bomb offices of a newspaper and a local bank[3]

-Jul 96: Phoenix, AR (near Luke AFB) – Federal agents arrest 12 militia members and seize 300 pounds of ammonium nitrate, 70 automatic rifles, thousands of rounds of ammunition and 200 blasting caps[4]

-Oct 96: Clarksburg, WV – The FBI arrested several militia members for allegedly plotting to bomb the FBI's Criminal Justice Information Services Facility[5]

-Apr 97: Yuba City, CA (near Beale AFB) – Police confiscate 550 pounds of a gelatin dynamite, allegedly stored by local militia activists; explosives are enough to destroy three city blocks

-Jul 97: Fort Hood, TX - Law enforcement officials interdicted a planned militia group attack on Fort Hood; militia members were arrested, and seizures included semiautomatic weapons and 1,600 rounds of ammunition[6]

Note: The perpetrators of this plot also considered Holloman AFB, NM, as a potential target due to the presence of foreign air force personnel at the base

-6 Mar 98: Holloman AFB, NM – Law enforcement personnel received information that a local militia group with an anti-foreign agenda might be targeting foreign personnel at the base

The above list should cast aside any thoughts USAF members might have that "terrorism can't happen here." Simply living on or near an USAF installation does not provide immunity from terrorism.

Recent Trends in CONUS Terrorism

In recent years, U.S. Government and security officials have expressed increased concern about the potential for an attack using weapons of mass destruction (WMD). An illustration of this concern is the 15 Mar 99, announcement by President Clinton approving the reallocation of $11 million in federal funds to bolster urban medical teams trained to respond to chemical and biological attacks.[7] Also, in 1999, the Health and Human Services Department will spend $158 million to prepare for possible bioterrorism and is asking for $230 million for the year 2000.[8] FBI statistics indicate the number of credible domestic threats involving WMD rose significantly in the first nine months of 1998. During that period the FBI opened more than 86 investigations into the threatened use of chemical, biological, radiological or nuclear materials.[9] The Pentagon has even established a new group, the Defense Threat Reduction Agency, to coordinate efforts against WMD threats.[10] Of particular concern to the group is the availability of WMD to small rogue nations and terrorist groups that transcend borders.[11]

While such attacks have fortunately not occurred to date, one problem that is happening with increasing frequency is telephonic or mailed threats of anthrax exposure. If inhaled and left untreated, anthrax spores can cause respiratory failure and death within a week (anthrax kills 80 percent of those people who inhale germ spores and are not treated[12]). In Dec 98 alone, Southern California experienced seven anthrax hoaxes.[13] These incidents included telephone threats to two Van Nuys courthouses that forced 1,500 people to be quarantined for several hours.[14] Even hoaxes can cause terror and pain as victims of a 22 Feb 99 anthrax hoax letter to a Planned Parenthood Clinic in Kansas City, Mo., learned. During this incident, twenty people had to be decontaminated with bleach and soapy water in a makeshift shower set up outside while a blizzard raged.[15] Other anthrax hoaxes have occurred in Colorado, Kentucky, Tennessee, Indiana, Georgia, and Washington, D.C., with 35 incidents reported in a five-day period between 18-22 Feb 99.[16]

It is only a matter of time before such threats are directed towards U.S. military resources. The potential dangers of anthrax exposure are so great that the Pentagon plans to inoculate all 2.4 million U.S. troops and reserves against anthrax exposure as a result of germ warfare.[17] While the anthrax threats so far have luckily been nuisances rather than actual attacks, they could have ominous implications. It is important to note that a typical terrorist modus operandi is to conduct probes of targets to test defenses for future attacks (such activity was observed before the Khobar Towers bombing). Additionally, such threats could at some point be used as a diversionary tactic for other criminal acts. It is too early to tell if these are simply hoaxes designed to cause disruption and fear or tests for further activities. One aspect is certain, whether a hoax or otherwise, intended victims must be prepared to confront these incidents and treat them as real attacks. Not to do so invites disaster.

Another trend is a tremendous rise in the number of domestic terrorism conspiracies that have been investigated since the Oklahoma City bombing. In a fall 1998 interview, Robert Blitzer, Chief of Domestic Terrorism and Counterterrorism Planning, stated that the FBI was running approximately 1,000 terrorism investigations, compared to about 100 before the Oklahoma attack.[18] A large portion of these cases are low level bombings that fall under the domestic terrorism mantle and have been linked in some way to a domestic terrorism group. On average, credible bomb threats arrive at government offices every two weeks.[19] To be sure, part of the rise in investigations can be attributed to increased resources (for instance, the FBI has recently hired several hundred new agents) and cooperation between federal, state, and local law enforcement. Still, whether caused by increased investigative resources, actual conspiracies, or copycat incidents, it is somewhat disconcerting that the FBI has so many open terrorist investigations.

As noted, some terrorist groups appear to be more willing to inflict mass casualties than they were in the past. Some experts believe that as the number of terrorist groups has declined, the hardcore element that remains are more serious and willing to conduct indiscriminate attacks. Individuals such as Timothy McVeigh and Osama bin Laden fit this description. In recent years, terrorist supporters in the U.S. have also improved their ability to collect information, raise money and issue rhetoric to gain publicity for their causes.[20]

A future trend to look for is increased terrorist group use of the Internet and potential cyber attacks against U.S government and military computer networks. In July 1998, CIA Director George Tenet stated that several countries, including some hostile to the U.S., are developing computer programs to attack other nation's information and computer systems.[21] Several international terrorist groups already have WebPages from which they solicit monetary contributions and spread propaganda regarding their causes. The Pentagon recently announced that its military computer systems are being subjected to ongoing, sophisticated and organized cyber-attacks that appear to be a concerted and coordinated effort from abroad.[22] Further, Pentagon computers are probed approximately 60 times per day with around 60 actual computer attacks each week.[23] While these incidents are probably the work of "normal" hackers (defined as people with no political/intelligence agenda) and intelligence agencies of foreign countries, as technology increases, the possibility of terror attacks via computer systems grows. In 1998, the Tamil Tiger terrorist group was credited with conducting a cyber attack against Sri Lankan government computer systems. Thus, there is precedent for terrorist attacks via cyberspace. Incidents such as these illustrate the need for USAF personnel and their dependents to practice good computer security measures (at work and at home) to avoid becoming victims.

Notes

[1] Terrorism Research Center, "Terrorist Intelligence Operations: A Renews Challenge for the Security Educator," [on line]; available from http://www.terrorism.com/terrorism/IntelOperations.html; Internet; accessed 13 Dec 98, 3.

[2] Ibid

[3] Kaplan, *Terrorism Threats at Home*, 25.

[4] Ibid.

[5] US Department of Justice, *Terrorism in the United States, 1996*, (Washington, D.C.: 1997), 7.

[6] Kaplan, *Terrorism Threats at Home*, 25.

[7] Associated Press, "Clinton takes aim at terrorist threat," *Montgomery Advertiser*, 16 Mar 99, sec A, 6A.

[8] CNN, "Senators urge government to stockpile anthrax, smallpox vaccines," [on line]; available from http://www.cnn.com/US/9903/17/PM-TerrorismThreat.ap/; Internet; accessed 17 Mar 99.

[9] Associated Press, "Security threats, checks increasing," *Montgomery Advertiser*, 3 Oct 98, sec A, 7A.

[10] Paul Levitt, "Anti-terrorism," *USA Today*, 2 Oct 98, sec A, 4A.

[11] Ibid.

[12] CNN, "Senators urge government to stockpile anthrax, smallpox vaccines."

[13] Associated Press, "800 quarantined after phony anthrax threat," *Montgomery Advertiser*, 29 Dec 98, sec A, 4A.

[14] CNN, "Southern California suffers fifth anthrax scare in a month," [on line]; available from http://www.cnn.com/US/9812/27/AM-AnthraxScare.ap/; Internet; accessed 28 Dec 98.

[15] T. Trent Gegax, "The New Bomb Threat," *Newsweek,* 22 Mar 99, 36.

[16] Ibid.

[17] CNN, "Senators urge government to stockpile anthrax, smallpox vaccines."

[18] Blitzer, "Fighting Terrorism: Leading FBI Official Discusses Domestic Terrorism," 2-3.

[19] Kaplan, *Terrorism Threats at Home*, 22.

[20] Federal Bureau of Investigation, "Terrorism: The Year in Review (1995)," [on line]; available from http://www.fbi.gov/publish/terror/year.htm; Internet; accessed 28 Sep 98.

[21] Educational Review, "CIA Warns Against Information Warfare," *Educational Review*, Sep/Oct 98, 10.

[22] Barbara Starr, "Pentagon Cyber-War," [on line] available from http://www.abcnews.go.com/sections/world/DailyNews/pentagonrussia88034.html; Internet; accessed 5 Mar 99.

[23] Ibid.

Chapter 4

The Issue of Security Awareness

The preceding chapters clearly illustrate the fact terrorist acts can, and do, occur inside the U.S. They also indicate the rising potential for increased CONUS terrorism in the future. Whether such terrorism will be directed against USAF installations is a matter open to discussion. However, one agreed upon way to decrease the potential for becoming the victim of terrorism is to present a strong security posture. Most terrorists will strike at less secure targets to increase their chances for success and escape. While the author applauds the fact most USAF installations have Security Forces troops manning base gates as an initial security precaution (as opposed to many U.S. Army installations which are open posts), additional measures are necessary to present the hardest possible target. If a terrorist group is committed to carrying out an attack, it *will* strike somewhere. For the USAF, the keys will be to make sure determined terrorists are interdicted or strike elsewhere.

Awareness plays an integral part in increasing the overall security environment at our USAF installations. Personnel security begins with the correct level of awareness concerning the threat environment.[1] Terrorists, and criminal elements for that matter, use overt and covert methods to collect intelligence from employees at the facilities they target.[2] The awareness of an alert Security Forces member helped save lives during the

Khobar Towers bombing. How many lives could have been saved if an alert citizen had noticed Timothy McVeigh conducting pre-operational surveillance activity prior to the Oklahoma City bombing? Obviously, not all terrorist acts can be prevented. Still, to counter such threats as much as possible, USAF personnel must believe a threat exists and realize that such collection occurs.

As terrorists employ new methods of attack and become more indiscriminate in their targeting, U.S. personnel will have to practice the best possible security awareness. Absent a full-scale terrorist campaign in the U.S., motivating people to take security awareness seriously will continue to be a challenge. The reluctance of individuals to take security precautions seriously is nicely illustrated by the story of a FBI SWAT team member who had deployed to Tanzania to help investigate the Embassy bombing last year. The individual failed to heed warnings about jogging along a beach area and was robbed at knifepoint by three youths.[3] If a trained professional will not follow security warnings in a high threat environment, how easy will it be to get the security awareness message across to laymen who live in a lower threat environment? With its briefing program that requires all personnel to receive an annual antiterrorism briefing, the Department of Defense has a vehicle for disseminating threat information. In fact, in 1998, AFOSI provided over 10,750 antiterrorism briefings. It is clear a lot of effort is being expended to get the message across to the USAF community. The key questions are how seriously do USAF personnel take these briefings and do they take the time to share security awareness information with their dependents?

An informal/unscientific survey the author conducted on two ACSC seminars reveals the potential problem of motivating USAF personnel to seriously consider security awareness practices. When asked what could be done to increase their awareness, one respondent only half-jokingly stated, "Frankly, I won't care until there's some terrorism near me." While this particular person ranks high on the cynical scale, the other responses indicated the need for security officials to make briefings and other antiterrorist initiatives personal. Given today's hectic environment, people have to be clearly shown how information and threats relate to them. It does not appear to be enough anymore to simply tell people a threat exists, it has to be proven to them before they will routinely consider security awareness issues. Hopefully steps can be taken to change this situation before a tragedy actually occurs.

A brief discussion to emphasize dependent awareness is warranted. The need for dependents to be aware of their surroundings and report suspicious activity is as critical as that for USAF personnel. Terrorists have in the past used dependents to collect targeting information for attacks against military members. Further, given the changing threat environment, dependents face much the same risks as their sponsors. It does not matter whether it is on a military installation or in the local community, good security awareness can help save lives. Thus, USAF personnel must ensure they talk about the local threat environment and awareness procedures with their families. Dependents must understand what to do with a suspicious package or envelope. Similarly, they must be informed how to handle suspicious requests for information, be they in person, by phone, or via the Internet. In short, the good security efforts of any particular USAF member could be wasted if they fail to similarly educate their dependents.

If awareness is so key, what can be done to increase it? Without a doubt, creative initiatives are needed. Receiving an annual briefing probably does not stimulate a large portion of the USAF population to practice higher levels of awareness. Per the previously mentioned informal ACSC survey, most respondents wanted to hear more information and see more pictures (including possibly short movies) about recent terrorist attacks. Some people wanted to be told about what type of terrorist indicators to look for and examples of preventive measures necessary to counter terrorist violence. Some even suggested AFOSI should stage mock terrorist attacks or leave fake bombs to show people their vulnerabilities. The consensus seemed to be that people need to be "scared" into taking potential threats seriously before they routinely contemplate security awareness practices.

Several awareness ideas that have been implemented at overseas USAF installations, could easily be benchmarked here in CONUS. Upon receipt of force protection information (could be about terrorist activity, demonstrations, criminal activity, etc.), the AFOSI detachment in Ankara, Turkey, circulates unclassified security awareness alerts via electronic mail to their base population. Leveraging technology in this way enabled the detachment to increase awareness much quicker than by past methods. Similar alert notices could be circulated via CONUS base networks. Further, quarterly security bulletins with awareness tips and terrorism indicators (among other topics) could also be circulated to augment the required annual briefing. While such bulletins at CONUS locations will never evoke the awareness levels found at high threat environments such as Turkey, they can reinforce past information. Also, even if only a few people internalize the information and increase their personal security awareness, the effort will be worthwhile.

Another positive initiative occurred at Incirlik Air Base, Turkey. Again, when threat information was received, the Wing Commander would convene a "Force Protection Town Meeting" to disseminate security information to the base population. In this manner, AFOSI could brief general information about the threat and put it into perspective to increase awareness while limiting paranoia and rumor. Perhaps such town meetings would be an initiative that more USAF commanders could use to share information about their local threat environment to their personnel. In addition, perhaps there might be some benefit in holding these meetings on a scheduled basis (i.e. quarterly or biannually) rather than holding the meetings on an as needed basis. Regular force protection discussions focused on the local threat environment and convened by senior commanders would help show the importance of high levels of security awareness. Even if the current local threat level is considered low, updated local threat information as well as national terrorist trends could be presented to sharpen USAF personnel focus regarding force protection issues. Undoubtedly a key to making such an initiative a success would be the support of senior base officials.

Creative use of computer networks has also helped spread the word about force protection issues. A growing number of bases, AFOSI detachments, and Security Force units are establishing WebPages that can be accessed by their community. Despite the man-hour cost of building and maintaining these sites, this effort must continue. Leveraging technology is essential to enhancing awareness in an era of limited resources. Establishing WebPages, maintaining current threat information (unclassified and classified depending on the computer systems available), and marketing the sites to the local populace can be a valuable tool for spreading the message of awareness.

An added bonus of these force protection initiatives to increase antiterrorist awareness is that alertness to other areas might also increase. For instance, people might also practice increased awareness regarding criminal matters (Note: this could flow both ways as increased awareness regarding criminal threats could foster increased awareness towards suspicious activities of terrorists). Also, those who practice proper security measures in CONUS are much more likely to practice such measures when serving overseas in generally higher threat environments. The goal should be to increase overall situational awareness to counter any type of potential threat. Law enforcement professionals largely depend on information from concerned citizens to help solve crimes. Increasing general threat awareness should translate into increased success in deterring crime as well.

As the new century dawns and new threats emerge, it will be incumbent upon USAF professionals, and Americans as well, to realize that such threats exist. The U.S. has not been, and will not be, immune from acts of devastation on our soil. Acceptance that threats exist and proper situational awareness will help USAF members protect themselves, their families and their friends. It might incur some monetary and man-hour costs to raise the awareness of all USAF personnel, but if one terrorist act is deterred or interdicted, those costs will be insignificant.

Notes

[1] Seger, *The Antiterrorism Handbook*, 35.
[2] Ibid, p. 63
[3] David E. Kaplan, "Welcome Wagon," *U.S. News and World Report*, 30 Nov 98, 12.

Chapter 5

Conclusion

This study has attempted to detail the antiterrorist challenges that the U.S. and the USAF in CONUS currently face and will continue to face in the future. With the presence of groups that have anti-government agendas, increased willingness to conduct larger scale attacks, and new technologies that enhance terrorist capabilities, the stakes of poor security awareness and practices continue to be raised. The new millennium will bring acts of terrorism to American cities and potentially to USAF installations. Preparation now will enhance the probability of deterring such attacks, and if a successful attack occurs, limit the cost in lives and resources. USAF personnel will have to decide if the cost of time and effort for security awareness initiatives is outweighed by the potential gains should CONUS-based USAF resources be targeted for attack. Current trends and future prospects for CONUS-based terrorism described in this paper clearly illustrate the potential cost of not practicing proper security awareness.

Increasing awareness and presenting the hardest possible target to those whom wish to do us harm will require the time, effort, and cooperation of all USAF personnel, from the Chief of Staff down to the newest airmen. Support from commanders, creativity by law enforcement, intelligence and security personnel, and perhaps most importantly, diligence by the USAF populace, are necessary ingredients to a successful antiterrorism program. Commanders have to set the standard for their troops and show security awareness matters. Law enforcement and security personnel have to continue their dedication to seeking creative ways of "get the message out," even if sometimes the efforts do not seem to be appreciated. Finally, USAF personnel, especially skeptical ones, must cast aside any ambivalence they have concerning this important topic. Terrorists rely on people to be ambivalent, lazy, predictable, and haphazard with their security practices. All USAF members should reevaluate their personnel security practices. If it takes spending a little time listening to a briefing, talking with AFOSI or other security personnel, reading a book, or conducting a little research on the Internet, the lives that might be saved could be your own or those of your family members.

Bibliography

Bodansky, Yossef. *Target the West: Terrorism in the World Today.* New York: Shapolsky Publishers, Inc., 1993.

Bolz, Frank, Dudonis, Kenneth J., and Schulz, David P *The Counterterrorism Handbook.* New York: Elsevier Science Publishing Co, Inc., 1990.

Bowman, Stephen. *When the Eagle Screams: America's Vulnerability to Terrorism.* New York: Carol Publishing Group, 1994.

CNN Interactive WebSite documents. [on line] Internet; available from: http://www.cnn.com, accessed Sep 98-Mar 99.

Educational Review, *CIA Warns Against Information Warfare*, Vol. 33, Issue 5, Sep/Oct 98.

Farrell, William R *The U.S. Government Response to Terrorism: In Search of an Effective Strategy.* Boulder, CO: Westview Press, 1982.

Heymann, Philip B. *Terrorism and America: A Commonsense Strategy for a Democratic Society.* Cambridge, Massachusetts: The MIT Press, 1998.

Hoffman, Bruce. *Inside Terrorism.* New York: Columbia University Press, 1998.

Kaplan, David E. "Terrorism Threat at Home." *U.S. News and World Report,* 29 December 1997, Vol 123, Issue 25.

Landay, Jonathan S. "As Radicalism Declines, Terrorism Surges." *Christian Science Monitor,* 20 August 1998, Vol 90, Issue 187.

Livingstone, Neil C., and Terrell E. Arnold. *Fighting Back: Winning the War Against Terrorism.* Lexington, Massachusetts: D.C. Heath and Company, 1984.

Montgomery Advertiser (Montgomery, AL). 3 Oct 1998 – 16 Mar 1999.

Morris, Eric and Hoe, Alan. *Terrorism: Threat and Response.* New York: St Martin's Press, 1988.

Newsweek. 22 Mar 99.

Rivers, Gayle. *The War Against Terrorists: How to Win It.* New York: Stein and Day Publishers, 1986.

Seger, Karl A. *The Antiterrorism Handbook.* Novato, CA: Presidio Press, 1990.

Smith, Brent L. *Terrorism in America: Pipe Bombs and Pipe Dreams.* New York: State University of New York Press, 1994.

Starr, Barbara, *Pentagon Cyber-War.* ABC News [on line], Internet: available from: http://abcnews.go.com/sections/world/DailyNews/pentagonrussia990304.html. Accessed 5 Mar 99

Southern Poverty Law Center studies, [on line] Internet: available from: http://www.splcenter.org, accessed Dec 98

The Terrorism Research Center. *Terrorist Intelligence Operations.* [on line] Internet: available from: http://www.terrorism.com/terrorism/IntelOperations.html

Tucker, H.H., ed. *Combating the Terrorists.* New York: Center for Security Studies, 1988.

USA Today (Arlington, VA). 23 Sep 98 – 31 Oct 98.

U.S. Congress. House. Military Research and Development Subcommittee. *The Federal Response to Domestic Terrorism Involving Weapons of Mass Destruction and the Status of the Department of Defense Support Program.* Report prepared by the U.S. Government Printing Office, 105th Congress 1st Sessions, Hearing Held 4 Nov 97.

U.S. Congress. House. Permanent Select Committee on Intelligence. *Terrorism – Looking Ahead: Issues and Options for Congress.* Report prepared by the Congressional Research Service, Library of Congress. 104th Congress, 2d Session, 1996.

U.S. Congress. Senate. Appropriations Committee Hearing on Counterterrorism. *Statement of Louis J. Freeh, Director Federal Bureau of Investigation Before the Senate Appropriations Committee Hearing on Counterterrorism.* 13 May 1997.

U.S. Congress. Senate. Judiciary Committee Subcommittee on Technology, Terrorism, and Government Information. *Statement of Dale Watson, Chief, International Terrorism Section, National Security Division, Federal Bureau of Investigation Before the Senate Judiciary Committee Subcommittee on Technology, Terrorism, and Government Information.* 24 February 1998.

U.S. Federal Bureau of Investigation. Counterterrorism Threat Assessment and Warning Unit, National Security Division. *Terrorism in the United States 1996.* Washington, D.C., 1996.

U.S. Federal Bureau of Investigation. Counterterrorism Threat Assessment and Warning Unit, National Security Division. *Terrorism in the United States 1995.* Washington, D.C., 1995.

U.S. News and World Report. 1997. 29 Dec; 1998. 5 Oct; 2, 30 Nov.

www.ingramcontent.com/pod-product-compliance
Lightning Source LLC
Chambersburg PA
CBHW052024280526
45793CB00005B/1114